Contents

U.S. Department of Housing and Urban Development

HUD's mission is to create strong, sustainable, inclusive communities and quality affordable homes for all. HUD is working to strengthen the housing market to bolster the economy and protect consumers, meet the need for quality affordable rental homes, utilize housing as a platform for improving quality of life, and build inclusive and sustainable communities free from discrimination. HUD grant resources typically fall into two basic categories: formula funds, distributed based on population and demographic data; and competitive grant funds, for which applicants compete.

Many HUD programs operate in rural as well as metropolitan areas, but funds might pass through state agencies or other entities to rural communities. HUD invests around $6.2 billion per year in rural areas. The majority of these funds provide affordable housing to low-income residents.

Community Planning and Development

HUD's Sustainable Communities Initiative provides competitive grants to support regional and local planning efforts that integrate housing, land use, economic and workforce development, transportation, and infrastructure investments in a manner that empowers jurisdictions to consider the interdependent challenges of economic competitiveness, social equity, access to opportunity, energy use, climate change, public health, and environmental protection. Its two primary grant programs, the Sustainable Communities Regional Planning Grant and Community Challenge Planning Grant programs, have both set aside funds for communities under 50,000 in population and regions below 200,000 in population. Funding was not appropriated for these programs in fiscal year 2012, but HUD is requesting $100 million to restore them in fiscal year 2013.

portal.hud.gov/hudportal/HUD?src=/program_offices/sustainable_housing_communities

- **Sustainable Communities Regional Planning Grants** support comprehensive metropolitan and multijurisdictional planning efforts that direct long-term regional development, address issues of regional significance, utilize data to set and monitor progress toward performance goals, and engage stakeholders and citizens in meaningful decision-making roles.

- **Community Challenge Planning Grants** support local efforts to update policies, codes, and capital investment plans to integrate transportation, housing, and economic development; support local real estate markets; and stimulate private investment. Projects can include amending or replacing local master plans, zoning codes, and building codes, either on a jurisdiction-wide basis or in a specific neighborhood, district, or corridor to promote mixed-use development, affordable housing, the reuse of older buildings and structures for new purposes, and main street and corridor revitalization.

Community Development Block Grants (CDBG) are flexible funding tools that address a wide range of community and economic development needs, including decent housing, healthy living environments, and expanded economic opportunity. Funds are allocated by a set formula directly to "entitlement communities," areas comprised of central cities of Metropolitan Statistical Areas, metropolitan cities with populations of at least 50,000, and qualified urban counties with populations of 200,000 or more (excluding the populations of entitlement cities). States typically distribute CDBG funds to rural counties (those with populations less than 200,000, excluding the populations of entitlement cities) and other areas not qualified as entitlement communities through a competitive process. Grant activities must benefit low- and moderate-income persons, aid in the prevention or elimination of slum and blight, or meet urgent community development needs.

Essex, Connecticut, courtesy of EPA

🖰 www.hud.gov/offices/cpd/communitydevelopment/programs

Section 108 is the loan guarantee provision of the CDBG program that provides public entities with loan funds to carry out economic development, housing, and public facility projects. The public entity may carry out the project itself or designate another public or nonprofit entity to do so. Section 108 loans are usually used by CDBG entitlement communities, but non-entitlement communities may also apply if their state agrees to pledge the CDBG funds necessary to secure the loan.

🖰 www.hud.gov/offices/cpd/communitydevelopment/programs/108/

Choice Neighborhoods builds off of the HOPE VI program, providing competitive grants to transform extremely poor neighborhoods with public and HUD-assisted housing into mixed-income communities with transportation options, employment and educational opportunities, and services. Planning Grants support the development of Transformation Plans that will guide the revitalization of public or HUD-assisted housing and surrounding neighborhoods. Implementation Grants support communities that are ready to implement their Transformation Plans, primarily funding the preservation and rehabilitation of public and HUD-assisted housing. Funding is available to public housing authorities working with local governments, nonprofit organizations, and for-profit developers.

🖰 portal.hud.gov/hudportal/HUD?src=/program_offices/public_indian_housing/programs/ph/cn

The Spokane Tribe of Indians in rural Eastern Washington received a HUD Community Challenge grant in 2010 to develop their first-ever community master plan. This opportunity to assess community needs led to greater, more informed participation in the regional economy through USDA Rural Development's Stronger Economies Together initiative. They've also been able to raise awareness about a new pilot public transit project to connect members with off-reservation job opportunities. In addition, having identified severe infrastructure needs through the HUD grant, they were able to receive Smart Growth Implementation Assistance from EPA to address failing water systems.

The Section 242 Hospital Mortgage Insurance Program provides mortgage insurance for loans originated by private lenders for acute care hospital facilities ranging from large teaching institutions to small rural critical access hospitals. Proposed projects are evaluated on the basis of whether they are acceptable insurance risks for the FHA Insurance Fund. This is not a competitive process.

> portal.hud.gov/hudportal/HUD?src=/federal_housing_administration/healthcare_facilities/section_242

Public Housing

The Public Housing program provides formula and competitive funding to local Public Housing Authorities (PHAs) for operating expenses and repairs to public housing developments. Funds are allocated based on the number of units PHAs own and their needs. PHAs are encouraged to use environmentally responsible practices through regulations, guidance, and incentive programs like Energy Performance Contracting, which provides funding to make public housing units more resource efficient through the implementation of energy and water conservation measures and the installation of renewable energy systems. www.hud.gov/offices/pih/programs/ph

> portal.hud.gov/hudportal/HUD?src=/program_offices/public_indian_housing/programs/ph/phecc/eperformance

Housing Choice and Project-Based Vouchers provide funding to PHAs for rental subsidies for units that are chosen by the tenant in the private market (Housing Choice Vouchers) or for use in specific developments or units (Project-Based Vouchers). Housing Choice Vouchers allow tenants more flexibility in deciding the location of their residence, giving them an opportunity to live closer to work, family, amenities, or services. The HUD Veterans Affairs Supportive Housing program provides additional vouchers specifically for veterans, which are combined with services provided by the Veterans' Administration.

> www.hud.gov/offices/pih/programs/hcv/about/index.cfm

Multifamily and Single Family Housing

HOME Investment Partnerships provide formula funding to states, cities, urban counties, and consortia (contiguous units of local governments with a binding agreement). Other localities may participate in HOME by applying for program funds made available by their state. Used to implement local housing strategies, the HOME program is designed to increase homeownership and affordable housing opportunities for low and very low-income Americans. Eligible uses of HOME funds include tenant-based rental assistance; rental and for-purchase housing rehabilitation; assistance to homebuyers; and new construction of rental and for-purchase housing. HOME funding may also be used for site acquisition, site improvements, demolition, relocation, and other activities.

       www.hud.gov/offices/cpd/affordablehousing/programs/home

Mortgage Insurance for Rental Housing insures lenders against loss on mortgage defaults related to the new construction and substantial rehabilitation of multifamily rental projects. HUD does not make direct loans, but provides mortgage insurance if the loan meets Federal Housing Administration (FHA) underwriting requirements. Several FHA programs provide this insurance to eligible owners and purchasers.

- Section 221(d)(4) and Section 221(d)(3) insure mortgage loans to facilitate the new construction or substantial rehabilitation of multifamily rental or cooperative housing for moderate-income families, elderly, and the handicapped. The former program can be used by for-profit sponsors and the latter by nonprofit sponsors.

         www.hud.gov/offices/hsg/mfh/progdesc/rentcoophsg221d3n4.cfm

- Section 207/223(f) insures mortgage loans to facilitate the purchase or refinancing of existing multifamily rental housing. Projects requiring substantial rehabilitation are not eligible for the program.

         www.hud.gov/offices/hsg/mfh/progdesc/purchrefi223f.cfm

The Housing Finance Agency Risk Sharing Program provides credit enhancement on loans underwritten and closed by a state or local housing finance agency. Eligible loans are for affordable housing including new construction, substantial rehabilitation, elderly housing, and refinancing. Owners and purchasers can apply for the program through the appropriate housing finance agency.

       www.hud.gov/offices/hsg/mfh/progdesc/riskshare542b.cfm

Local Home Buying Programs are provided directly or financially supported by HUD to promote and support homeownership. These include FHA mortgage insurance, housing counseling, and the sale of HUD-owned property.

       www.hud.gov/buying/localbuying.cfm and

       portal.hud.gov/hudportal/HUD?src=/topics/owning

203(b) Mortgage Insurance insures loans originated by FHA-approved lenders to finance the purchase or refinancing of a home or condominium with up to four dwelling units serving as the principal residence of the borrower.

       portal.hud.gov/hudportal/HUD?src=/program_offices/housing/sfh/ins/sfh203b

The 203(k) Rehabilitation Mortgage Insurance program is HUD's primary mechanism for the rehabilitation of single family properties. It insures loans originated by FHA-approved lenders to finance acquisitions and rehabilitations of single family properties with up to four dwelling units that have been completed for at least one year.

       portal.hud.gov/hudportal/HUD?src=/program_offices/housing/sfh/203k/203kabou

Title I Home Improvement Loans are originated by FHA-approved lenders and insured by HUD. Loans for single-family homes can be used for alterations, repairs, and site improvements. Loans for multifamily structures can be used only for building alteration and repairs.

       portal.hud.gov/hudportal/HUD?src=/program_offices/housing/sfh/title/ti_abou

Home Mortgage and Foreclosure Counseling is sponsored by HUD to provide free or low-cost advice on buying or renting a home, avoiding mortgage default and foreclosure, and dealing with credit issues. Tenants, homeowners, or homebuyers can receive counseling from HUD-approved and HUD-funded counseling agencies in their states.

       portal.hud.gov/hudportal/HUD?src=/i_want_to/talk_to_a_housing_counselor

       www.hud.gov/offices/hsg/sfh/hcc/hcs.cfm

Fair Housing

The Fair Housing Initiatives Program funds fair housing organizations and other nonprofits to assist people who believe they have been victims of housing discrimination. These organizations conduct preliminary investigations of discrimination claims and help people identify government agencies that handle complaints of housing discrimination.

> portal.hud.gov/hudportal/HUD?src=/program_offices/fair_housing_equal_opp/partners/FHIP

The Fair Housing Assistance Program provides funding on a noncompetitive basis to state and local agencies that enforce fair housing laws that are substantially equivalent to the federal Fair Housing Act. This program supports a variety of fair housing administrative and enforcement activities, including complaint processing, training, the development of data and information systems, and other projects.

> portal.hud.gov/hudportal/HUD?src=/program_offices/fair_housing_equal_opp/partners/FHAP

Tribes

The Indian Community Development Block Grant Program provides grants to develop decent housing, suitable living environments, and economic opportunities for low- and moderate-income persons in Indian and Alaska Native communities. Eligible applicants include any Indian tribe, band, group, or nation or Alaska Native village which has established a relationship with the federal government as defined in the program regulations. Funds can be used for housing rehabilitation, land acquisition for new housing construction, the construction of community infrastructure such as roads and water and sewer facilities, community buildings, and commercial, industrial, and agricultural projects.

> portal.hud.gov/hudportal/HUD?src=/program_offices/public_indian_housing/ih/grants/icdbg

The Indian Housing Block Grant Program is a formula grant program that funds a range of affordable housing activities in Indian reservations and Indian areas. Eligible recipients are federally recognized Indian tribes or their tribally designated housing entities, as well as a limited number of state-recognized tribes formerly eligible under the United States Housing Act of 1937. Eligible activities include housing development, assistance for housing developed under the Indian Housing Program, housing services to eligible families and individuals, crime prevention and safety, and model activities that highlight creative approaches to solving affordable housing problems.

> portal.hud.gov/hudportal/HUD?src=/program_offices/public_indian_housing/ih/grants/ihbg

The Title VI Tribal Housing Activities Loan Guarantee Program provides loan guarantees for Indian Housing Block Grant recipients who need additional funds to carry out eligible affordable housing activities but are unable to borrow from other sources without the guarantee of payment by the federal government.

> portal.hud.gov/hudportal/HUD?src=/program_offices/public_indian_housing/ih/homeownership/titlevi/

The Section 184 Indian Home Loan Guarantee Program gives Native Americans access to private mortgage financing by providing loan guarantees to lenders. Section 184 covers family homes located in an Indian or Alaska Native area where the land is tribal trust, allotted individual trust, or fee simple.

> portal.hud.gov/hudportal/HUD?src=/program_offices/public_indian_housing/ih/homeownership/184

Supportive Housing for Target Populations

Mortgage Insurance for Residential Care Facilities is provided on loans made by FHA-approved lenders to purchase, refinance, construct, or rehabilitate housing for the frail elderly in need of supportive services. This type of housing can include nursing homes, assisted living facilities, and board and care facilities. Proposed projects are evaluated on the basis of whether they are acceptable insurance risks for the FHA Insurance Fund. This is not a competitive process.

> portal.hud.gov/hudportal/HUD?src=/federal_housing_administration/healthcare_facilities/section_232/lean_processing_page

The Section 202 Supportive Housing for the Elderly and Section 811 Supportive Housing for Persons with Disabilities programs provide competitive funding to nonprofit agencies developing and operating housing for the elderly and persons with disabilities. Funds can support original construction and rental assistance to ensure that rents remain affordable to very low-income people.

> www.hud.gov/offices/hsg/mfh/progdesc/eld202.cfm
> www.hud.gov/offices/hsg/mfh/progdesc/disab811.cfm

Housing Opportunities for Persons with AIDS provides formula funding and limited competitive grants to states, cities, and nonprofit organizations to develop housing and supportive services for people with AIDS.

> www.hud.gov/offices/cpd/aidshousing/index.cfm

Homeless Programs provide formula and competitive funding to state and local governments and nonprofit organizations that offer housing, homeless prevention programs, rental assistance, and other supportive services to families and individuals facing a housing crisis or homelesness.

> portal.hud.gov/hudportal/HUD?src=/program_offices/comm_planning/homeless

Healthy Homes

The Lead Hazard Control Grant Program provides competitive grants to state, local, and tribal governments to identify and control lead-based paint hazards in privately-owned rental or owner-occupied housing.

> portal.hud.gov/hudportal/HUD?src=/program_offices/healthy_homes/lbp/lhc

U.S. Department of Transportation

DOT is supporting livable and sustainable rural and tribal communities through the TIGER discretionary grant program, investments in public transit projects, and other Federal Highway Administration (FHWA) and Federal Transit Administration (FTA) programs described here. These programs can help rural communities enhance access to affordable housing, improve safety on rural roads, increase the efficiency of freight movement, strengthen economic competitiveness, and protect the environment. Since the majority of federal transportation funding is distributed to states and transit agencies through formula programs, communities can access these programs by working closely with their state departments of transportation.

The information listed here will change after October 1, 2012 due to the new transportation authorization. For a full description of DOT funding, see www.dot.gov.

Planning and Capacity Building

State Planning and Research formula funds may be used for engineering and economic surveys and investigations; physical and financial planning of highway programs and local public transportation systems; research, development, and technology transfer activities related to the planning, design, construction, management, and maintenance of highway, public transportation, and intermodal transportation systems; and studies, research, and training on engineering standards and construction materials.

  www.fhwa.dot.gov/federalaid/guide/guide_current.cfm#c76

The FHWA/FTA Transportation Planning Capacity Building Program seeks to recognize, support, and promote effective statewide, metropolitan, and rural transportation planning practices nationwide by providing opportunities for sharing solutions throughout the professional planning community. The program offers information, classroom and web-based training, scenario planning workshops, and technical assistance to transportation planning professionals.

  www.planning.dot.gov/

The program's website features a Rural and Small Community Planning page with links to publications, legislation and guidance, upcoming events, and related websites.

  www.planning.dot.gov/focus_rural.asp

The Surface Transportation Environment and Planning Cooperative Research Program aims to improve the understanding of the relationship between surface transportation and the environment. Under this program FHWA builds capacity through activities such as scenario planning, peer exchanges, research, and other activities.

  www.fhwa.dot.gov/federalaid/guide/guide_current.cfm#c77

Multimodal Transportation

TIGER (Transportation Investment Generating Economic Recovery) Discretionary Grants fund innovative transportation projects that will create jobs and have a significant impact on the nation, a region, or a metropolitan area. Grants support projects from state and local governments that improve the condition of existing facilities, contribute to the country's economic competitiveness, foster livable communities, and improve energy efficiency and safety. Past rounds of TIGER grants have set aside funding for projects in rural areas.

> www.dot.gov/tiger/index.html

Surface Transportation Program formula funds can be used for highway and transit infrastructure construction and rehabilitation, highway operational improvements such as hazard elimination, bicycle and pedestrian transportation infrastructure, transportation planning, highway and transit research and development and technology transfer programs, and capital and operating costs for traffic monitoring, management, and control facilities and programs, including advanced truck stop electrification systems.

> www.fhwa.dot.gov/federalaid/guide/guide_current.cfm#c78

Virginia, courtesy of EPA

The Congestion Mitigation and Air Quality Improvement Program funds projects in nonattainment areas for air quality standards. Eligible projects include pedestrian and bicycle facilities; transit facilities; the implementation of traffic management, monitoring, and congestion relief strategies; alternative fuel projects; vehicle inspection and maintenance programs; intermodal freight; travel demand management; rideshare programs; and others that can help improve air quality.

> www.fhwa.dot.gov/federalaid/guide/guide_current.cfm#c08

The Public Lands Highways program provides funding for transportation planning, research, and engineering; construction of highways, roads, and transit facilities; and the operation and maintenance of transit facilities on public lands, national parks, and Indian reservations.

> www.fhwa.dot.gov/federalaid/guide/guide_current.cfm#c57a

The Recreational Trails Program provides formula funds to states to develop and maintain recreational trails and facilities for non-motorized and motorized recreational uses such as hiking, bicycling, in-line skating, equestrian use, cross-country skiing, snowmobiling, off-road motorcycling, and all-terrain vehicle riding.

    🖱   www.fhwa.dot.gov/environment/recreational_trails/index.cfm

The Transportation Enhancement Activities Program offers formula funding to expand transportation choices. There are 12 eligible activities, including pedestrian and bicycle infrastructure and safety programs, scenic and historic highway programs, landscaping and scenic beautification, historic preservation, and environmental mitigation.

    🖱   www.fhwa.dot.gov/environment/transportation_enhancements/

The Safe Routes to School Program helps communities make walking and bicycling to school a safe and convenient activity by providing formula funding for a wide variety of infrastructure and non-infrastructure projects, from building safer street crossings to establishing programs that encourage children and their parents to walk and bicycle to school.

    🖱   safety.fhwa.dot.gov/saferoutes/

Public Transit

Formula Grants for Other than Urbanized Areas (5311) provide funding to states to support public transportation in rural areas with populations less than 50,000. Funding can be used to assist in the maintenance, development, improvement, and use of public transportation systems.

    🖱   www.fta.dot.gov/grants/13093_3555.html

The Paul S. Sarbanes Transit in the Parks Discretionary Grant Program protects environmentally sensitive national parks, national forests, wildlife refuges, and other federal lands while improving the visitor experience by funding transit and non-motorized transportation. Administered by FTA in partnership with the Department of the Interior and the Forest Service, the program funds capital and planning expenses for transportation alternatives such as shuttle buses and bicycle trails on public lands and in the surrounding communities.

    🖱   www.fta.dot.gov/funding/grants/grants_financing_6106.html

National RTAP offers a comprehensive array of free training and technical assistance resources for rural, small urban, and tribal transit operators that help to strengthen their transit services and contribute to the sustainability of their communities.

Using National RTAP resources, transit providers can supplement or revamp their training programs; find news, answers, events, and peer assistance; manage federally funded procurement with ProcurementPRO; create a website with Website Builder; and prepare bus route and schedule data for Google Transit or other online trip planners with GTFS Builder.

Examples of technical assistance from National RTAP have included:

- Aid with the design of a community survey for a transit planning grant in the native village of Fort Yukon, AK
- Information about potential funding sources and planning assistance to start a transit system in the native village of Point Hope, AK
- Assistance with a Tribal Transit Program grant application to the Bois Forte Band of Chippewa, MN

The Bus and Bus Facilities Discretionary Grant Program provides capital assistance for new and replacement buses and related equipment and facilities including intermodal transit centers. Funding is available to states for projects in rural and small urban areas below 200,000 in population.

      www.fta.dot.gov/funding/grants/grants_financing_3557.html

The Rural Transit Assistance Program provides funding to states to assist in the design and implementation of training and technical assistance projects and other support services for transit operators in non-urbanized areas with populations under 50,000. The program also provides national technical assistance resources and a peer-to-peer network that connects professionals from across the country, allowing them to work together to address challenges, identify opportunities, and share best practices (see text box, next page).

      www.fta.dot.gov/funding/grants/grants_financing_3554.html

Streets and Highways

The Transportation, Community, and System Preservation Program provides discretionary funding to states, metropolitan planning organizations, local governments, and tribal governments to plan and implement strategies that improve the efficiency of the transportation system, reduce its environmental impact, ensure efficient access to jobs and services, and promote development patterns that advance these goals.

      www.fhwa.dot.gov/tcsp/projects.html

The Colorado Department of Local Affairs received a TIGER II Planning Grant and a HUD Community Challenge Grant to help three small communities—Fowler, Monte Vista, and Rifle—pursue a unique joint planning initiative to revitalize their downtowns. The work will include creating construction-ready design drawings for the renovation of historic buildings and planning for development that will increase walkability, transportation choice, and energy efficiency.

Interstate Maintenance provides formula funding for Interstate resurfacing, restoration, rehabilitation, and reconstruction; the reconstruction or new construction of bridges, interchanges, and crossings; capital costs related to operational, safety, traffic management, or intelligent transportation systems improvements; and preventive maintenance.

    www.fhwa.dot.gov/federalaid/guide/guide_current.cfm#c42

The Highway Safety Improvement Program aims to reduce traffic fatalities and serious injuries on public roads and publicly owned bicycle and pedestrian pathways. States must develop and implement Strategic Highway Safety Plans, produce a program of projects or strategies based on data analysis, evaluate the plans on a regular basis, and submit annual reports to DOT in order to obligate the formula funds received through this program.

    www.fhwa.dot.gov/federalaid/guide/guide_current.cfm#c30

The Highway Bridge Program provides formula funding to improve structurally deficient and functionally obsolete highway bridges on public roads.

    www.fhwa.dot.gov/federalaid/guide/guide_current.cfm#c29

National Scenic Byways Program funds may be used for projects along All-American Roads, National Scenic Byways, State scenic byways, and tribal scenic byways and for the planning and development of state or tribal scenic byways programs. Eligible projects include safety improvements to scenic byways; construction of facilities for pedestrians and bicyclists, rest area turnouts, overlooks, and interpretive facilities; highway improvements that improve access to recreation; and scenic byways marketing plans and programs.

    www.bywaysonline.org/

The High Risk Rural Roads Program aims to reduce traffic fatalities and injuries on rural roads. Formula funds can be used to carry out construction and operational improvements on roadways classified as rural collectors or local roads where accident rates exceed the statewide average.

    www.fhwa.dot.gov/federalaid/guide/guide_current.cfm#c28

Tribes

The Public Transportation on Indian Reservations Discretionary Grant Program provides funding to federally-recognized Indian tribes based on an annual competitive selection process. Grant recipients can use funds for planning, capital, and operating assistance for rural transit services, including intercity bus service.

     www.fta.dot.gov/funding/grants/grants_financing_3553.html

Supportive Services for Target Populations

The Transportation for Elderly Persons and Persons with Disabilities Program provides formula funding to states to help nonprofit groups meet the transportation needs of the elderly and persons with disabilities when transportation service is unavailable or insufficient.

     www.fta.dot.gov/funding/grants/grants_financing_3556.html

The Job Access and Reverse Commute Program provides formula funding to states and other public bodies towards capital, planning, and operating expenses for projects that transport low-income individuals and students to and from jobs, employment centers, and educational institutions.

     www.fta.dot.gov/funding/grants/grants_financing_3550.html

The New Freedom Formula Grant Program aims to help overcome barriers that Americans with disabilities face related to workforce participation and transportation access. It provides formula funding to states and other public bodies towards capital and operating expenses for new public transportation services and alternatives beyond those required by the American with Disabilities Act that are designed to assist individuals with disabilities.

     www.fta.dot.gov/funding/grants/grants_financing_3549.html

The National Resource Center for Human Service Transportation Coordination offers technical assistance resources, trainings, coordination ambassadors, and other resources to help states and communities integrate public transportation and human services networks. The Center is funded through a cooperative agreement with FTA.

     www.unitedweride.gov/1_10_ENG_HTML.htm

The National Center on Senior Transportation is a training and technical assistance project that aims to increase transportation options for older adults and enhance their ability to live independently. The Center is funded through a cooperative agreement with FTA and the Administration on Aging.

     seniortransportation.easterseals.com/site/PageServer?pagename=NCST2_homepage

Lewes, Delaware, courtesy of EPA

Easter Seals Project ACTION (Accessible Community Transportation in Our Nation) is a national technical assistance project to encourage and facilitate cooperation between the disability and transportation communities, with the goal of achieving universal access to transportation for persons with disabilities nationwide. This project is funded through a cooperative agreement with FTA.

  projectaction.easterseals.com/site/PageServer?pagename=ESPA_homepage

The National Joblinks Employment Transportation Initiative, a program of the Community Transportation Association of America, provides training, educational workshops, conferences, interagency action planning events, publications, and knowledge-sharing opportunities to help communities overcome transportation barriers preventing low-income individuals from getting and keeping jobs. It is funded by DOT and the U.S. Department of Labor.

  web1.ctaa.org/webmodules/webarticles/anmviewer.asp?a=17&z=40

U.S. Environmental Protection Agency

EPA's mission is to protect public health and the environment, and creating safe, healthy, and livable communities is a key part of that. The agency offers a variety of grant, technical assistance, and capacity-building programs to help communities clean up pollution and prepare contaminated sites for development; build water infrastructure, including green infrastructure; increase energy efficiency; and implement smart growth approaches to development that expand economic opportunity, protect clean air and water, and enhance residents' quality of life. Some of these programs are described here. The majority are awarded on a competitive basis. Some of them provide direct funding to communities while others deliver technical assistance services and not monetary awards. While the majority of EPA programs do not formally set aside funds for rural communities, they are at work in many rural places.

Community Planning

The Smart Growth Implementation Assistance Program provides technical assistance to state, local, regional, and tribal governments that want to develop in ways that protect the environment, use resources efficiently, create economic opportunities, and provide good quality of life. National experts work with selected communities to explore barriers to smart growth implementation and pilot innovative approaches to development.

www.epa.gov/smartgrowth/sgia.htm

The Building Blocks for Sustainable Communities Program provides quick, targeted technical assistance to communities using a variety of tools that have demonstrated results and widespread application. Tools, delivered by experts at one day workshops, include walking audits, rural and small town zoning evaluations, and complete streets assessments. This assistance helps selected local and tribal governments overcome common land use challenges and implement development approaches that expand economic opportunity, protect the environment, improve public health, and enhance quality of life. The Building Blocks program is geared toward communities that are relatively new to smart growth but have a basic understanding of the concepts and how they apply locally.

www.epa.gov/smartgrowth/buildingblocks.htm

The Governors' Institute on Community Design assists governors and state leaders as they make investments in their communities and guide growth and development in their states. The Institute brings together leading practitioners and academicians in key fields, including land use policy, design, transportation, energy, development, and economics, for a two-day workshop with the state's executive team that is tailored to the needs of the state. Governors' Institute technical assistance is designed to provide state leaders with practical strategies to create vibrant, economically competitive communities; highlight the connections between economic development, transportation, land use, housing, energy and the environment; bring together a broad range of decision-makers to catalyze coordinated action among state agencies; and encourage increased cooperation between state and local governments. EPA supports the Governors' Institute through a cooperative agreement.

🖰 www.govinstitute.org/

Brownfields Cleanup and Redevelopment

EPA has a variety of programs to help communities assess, remediate, and restore brownfield sites to productive use and revitalize affected neighborhoods. Brownfields are properties whose expansion, redevelopment, or reuse might be complicated by the presence or potential presence of a hazardous substance, pollutant, or contaminant. For more information, see www.epa.gov/brownfields. Proposal and funding information for available brownfields grants can be found at www.epa.gov/brownfields/applicat.htm

Victor and Driggs, Idaho: Using EPA Technical Assistance to Meet Local Goals

Victor and Driggs, two rapidly growing small towns in Idaho's Teton Valley, received EPA's Smart Growth Implementation Assistance in 2006. The communities asked the EPA-led team to provide policy options that would enhance the Valley's unique character, promote thriving downtown districts with opportunities for local and regional retail, and create safe and attractive pedestrian environments.

The project focused on Highway 33, which serves as a main street and a busy regional transportation corridor through both towns. The team proposed several options for slowing traffic speeds and making the downtown portions of the highway safer and more inviting for pedestrians, including separating local traffic from through traffic, separating lanes with medians that could be used as pedestrian refuges, and providing on-street parking.

The City of Victor found a way to begin implementing these concepts with minimal funding. They worked with the Idaho Transportation Department to add bike lanes and diagonal parking spaces, narrowing travel lanes, calming traffic, and increasing transportation options for residents and customers of local businesses. This simple investment set the stage for attracting the downtown activity that residents want and demonstrated to developers that revitalization is a priority for the City. Through its Envision Victor effort, the community is exploring other ways of implementing the options presented by the technical assistance.

When looking to expand the local school system, Western North Carolina's Henderson County and the Town of Fletcher chose a 28-acre former log home manufacturing facility site. However, the town soon learned that the site was contaminated with dioxin and pentachlorophenol (PCP) and was not suitable for a school.

The town shifted its vision to creating a vibrant downtown area on the site—the "Heart of Fletcher"—as the widening of Highway 25 had displaced the original downtown in 2003. Through an intensive public process, the town of 4,200 people crafted a Strategic Plan that outlined a vision of a walkable downtown with a city hall, municipal buildings, small business, residences, and walking trails.

The Town of Fletcher worked with the Land of Sky Regional Council (LOSRC) to obtain an EPA brownfields cleanup grant of $200,000 and a $50,000 subgrant from the LOSRC Revolving Loan Fund Program, which is funded by EPA. The contaminated soil has been removed, clean fill has been added, and ground water is monitored annually to ensure its safety.

The town rezoned the site for downtown development, put property tax incentives in place to attract developers, and received a $350,000 grant from the North Carolina Department of Transportation to build an access road. Additionally, the town was awarded a $5 million Community Facilities loan from USDA Rural Development to construct a 25,400-square foot Town Hall and Public Safety Building to anchor the Heart of Fletcher district.

Assessment Grants can be used to inventory, characterize, assess, and conduct planning and community involvement related to brownfield sites.

> www.epa.gov/brownfields/assessment_grants.htm

Cleanup Grants provide funding for a recipient to carry out cleanup activities at brownfield sites that it owns.

> www.epa.gov/brownfields/cleanup_grants.htm

Revolving Loan Fund Grants provide funding to capitalize a revolving loan fund. Revolving loan funds can be used to provide no-interest or low-interest loans and subgrants to eligible entities to carry out cleanup activities at brownfield sites that they own.

> www.epa.gov/brownfields/rlflst.htm

State and Tribal Response Programs oversee assessment and cleanup activities at the majority of brownfield sites across the country. This non-competitive grant program can support the development of a response program's regulations or procedures, the purchase of environmental insurance, the capitalization of a Revolving Loan Fund for brownfields cleanup, and other activities. Funding goes directly to states and tribes. Depending on state and tribal priorities, communities may be able to access some of the funding for their own environmental insurance, technical assistance, or other capital needs.

Chapel Hill, North Carolina, courtesy of EPA

⌐ô   www.epa.gov/brownfields/state_tribal/

Brownfields Area-Wide Planning Grants help communities develop brownfield reuse plans and implementation strategies for an area, such as a neighborhood, commercial corridor or downtown district, with multiple brownfield sites.

⌐ô   www.epa.gov/brownfields/areawide_grants.htm

Brownfields Environmental Workforce Development and Job Training Grants provide funding to local and state governments, land clearance authorities and other quasi-governmental entities, regional councils and groups of local governments, nonprofit organizations, and others to help communities take advan¬tage of the jobs created by the assessment and cleanup of brownfields. The grants prepare and place unemployed and underemployed, predominantly low-income and minority residents in jobs in the environmental field and in the brownfields assessment and cleanup work taking place in their communities.

⌐ô   www.epa.gov/brownfields/job.htm

Targeted Brownfields Assessments, conducted by EPA contractors, can include site assessments, analyses of cleanup options and cost estimates, and community outreach. Sites for this program are selected by EPA regional offices. This program delivers services, not funding.

⌐ô   www.epa.gov/brownfields/grant_info/tba.htm

Technical Assistance to Brownfields (TAB) Communities services are provided to local and state governments, regional entities, and other stakeholders that need technical assistance dealing with brownfield sites. The program can also assist communities with applying for EPA brownfields grants or identifying other resources to address their brownfield sites. Most TAB services are provided free of charge, but applicants should check with the TAB provider in their region. Some of the TAB providers make concerted efforts to serve rural communities. This program does not deliver direct funding to communities.

⌐ᐤ   epa.gov/brownfields/tools/tab_bifold.pdf

Water Infrastructure and Water Quality

The **Clean Water State Revolving Fund (CWSRF)** and **Drinking Water State Revolving Fund (DWSRF)** Programs provide permanent sources of low-cost financing for a range of water quality infrastructure projects such as traditional wastewater treat¬ment and collection, nonpoint source and estuary management, green infrastructure, and capital improvements to public drinking water systems. Funds to capitalize the revolving funds are provided annually through federal grants and state matching funds. Monies are loaned to assistance recipients at below-market rates, and states have the ability to customize loan terms to benefit small and disadvantaged communities. Loan repayments are recycled back into the revolving funds to be used for additional projects. Eligible loan recipients vary by program and by state. Since their inception, the CWSRF and DWSRF programs have provided over $111 billion in assistance to borrowers including communities of all sizes, farmers, homeowners, small businesses, and nonprofit organizations.

⌐ᐤ   water.epa.gov/grants_funding/cwsrf/cwsrf_index.cfm

⌐ᐤ   www.epa.gov/safewater/dwsrf/

The **U.S.-Mexico Border Water Infrastructure Grant Program** provides grants for the planning, design, and construction of high priority wastewater and drinking water facilities to communities within 100 km (approximately 62 miles) north and south of the U.S.-Mexico Border.

⌐ᐤ   www.epa.gov/Border2012/infrastructure/

Nonpoint Source Implementation Grants help states and tribes reduce nonpoint source pollution. These grants support state and tribal programs and projects, and most states and tribes provide project funds through a competitive process to organizations and local governments. Projects have included activities related to agriculture, ground water protection, forestry, urban storm water runoff, and others.

⌐ᐤ   www.epa.gov/nps/cwact.html

The **Pollution Control Grant Program (Clean Water Act Section 106)** provides grants to states, interstate agencies, and eligible federally-recognized Indian tribes to assist in the development and implementation of water pollution control programs. Grants may be used to fund water quality planning and assessments, the development of water quality standards, ground water and wetland protection, nonpoint source control, and other activities.

⌐ᐤ   water.epa.gov/grants_funding/cwf/pollutioncontrol.cfm

Green Infrastructure Funding Resources: Green infrastructure approaches infiltrate, capture, evapotranspire, and reuse stormwater to reduce polluted runoff, protect water quality, and make neighborhoods safer, healthier, and more attractive. EPA has compiled a list of funding resources to help communities fund green infrastructure projects.

   water.epa.gov/infrastructure/greeninfrastructure/gi_funding.cfm

Tribes

The Alaska Native Village and Rural Communities Sanitation Grant Program provides grants to Alaska Native Villages and rural Alaskan communities for the planning, design, and construction of new drinking water and wastewater treatment systems and improvements in existing systems, as well as for training and technical assistance in system operations and maintenance.

   www.epa.gov/owm/mab/indian/anvrs.htm

The Clean Water Indian Set-Aside Program, administered in cooperation with the Indian Health Service, provides grants for the planning, design, and construction of wastewater infrastructure to federally recognized Indian tribes and Alaska Native Villages. EPA uses Indian Health Service priority lists to identify and select projects to be funded. To be considered for funding, tribes must identify their wastewater needs to the Indian Health Service.

   water.epa.gov/type/watersheds/wastewater/Clean-Water-Indian-Set-Aside-Grant-Program.cfm

The U.S.-Mexico Tribal Border Infrastructure Grant Program provides grants to federally-recognized tribes whose reservations are within 100 km (approximately 62 miles) north of the U.S.-Mexico border for the planning, design, and construction of high priority drinking water and wastewater infrastructure projects.

   www.epa.gov/Border2012/infrastructure/

Environmental Justice

Environmental justice is the fair treatment and meaningful involvement of all people regardless of race, color, national origin, or income with respect to the development, implementation, and enforcement of environmental laws, regulations, and policies. For more information, see www.epa.gov/environmentaljustice/.

The Environmental Justice Small Grants Program provides financial assistance to eligible nonprofit organizations and tribal governments to build collaborative partnerships, identify local environmental and public health issues, envision solutions, and empower the community through education, training, and outreach.

   www.epa.gov/environmentaljustice/grants/ej-smgrants.html

The Environmental Justice Collaborative Problem-Solving Cooperative Agreement Program
provides financial assistance to eligible community-based organizations working on or planning to
work on projects to address local environmental and public health issues using EPA's Environmental
Justice Collaborative Problem-Solving Model.

   www.epa.gov/environmentaljustice/grants/ej-cps-grants.html

Healthy Buildings

The State Indoor Radon Grant Program provides grant funds to states and tribes to help finance
radon risk reduction programs. These programs should aim to help builders, property owners, non-
governmental organizations, radon services professionals, and others construct new homes and
schools to include radon-reducing features and reduce radon levels in existing homes and schools.

   www.epa.gov/radon/sirgprogram.html

Energy Efficiency

Along with the resources described here, the U.S. Department of Energy (which is not a member
of the Partnership for Sustainable Communities) also offers a variety of energy efficiency assistance
opportunities.

The Local Climate and Energy Program helps local governments meet multiple environmental
and economic goals with cost-effective climate change mitigation and clean energy strategies.
EPA provides local governments with peer exchange training opportunities along with planning,
policy, technical, and analytical
information that supports reduction
of greenhouse gas emissions.

   www.epa.gov/
statelocalclimate

Starkville, Mississippi, courtesy of EPA

**The ENERGY STAR for New Homes
Program** certifies new homes that
meet certain energy efficiency
standards. Builders sign on as
partners with EPA and then work
with certified experts to incorporate
energy-efficient features into their
homes.

   www.energystar.gov/

U.S. Department of Agriculture

USDA's historic and extensive presence in rural America provides rich opportunities for supporting community and economic development, improving housing options, and strengthening local and regional food systems. USDA programs can help implement the community plans funded by the Partnership agencies, which is particularly important in small communities that may lack the resources and capacity to put their visions and goals into practice.

Community and Economic Development

The Community Facilities Program provides loans, loan guarantees, and grants for the construction, acquisition, or renovation of community facilities and for the purchase of equipment for those facilities, which can include schools, hospitals, community centers, emergency response services, and a wide variety of others.

In Wrangell, Alaska, an island community with limited access to fresh food, the Wrangell Medical Center received a Community Facilities grant of $100,000 to purchase two greenhouses for a community garden.

> www.rurdev.usda.gov/HCF_CF.html

The Rural Community Development Initiative provides grants and technical assistance to develop the capacity of nonprofit community-based housing and community development organizations and low-income communities in rural areas to improve housing and community facilities and undertake community and economic development projects.

> www.rurdev.usda.gov/HAD-RCDI_Grants.html

Business Development

The Business and Industry Guaranteed Loan Program provides guarantees on loans made by private lenders to help new and existing businesses in rural areas gain access to affordable capital. By issuing a guarantee, USDA essentially co-signs the loan with the recipient, lowering the lender's risk and allowing for more favorable interest rates and terms. The 2008 Farm Bill placed a special emphasis on supporting businesses that facilitate the processing, distribution, aggregation, storing, and marketing of locally or regionally produced foods.

> www.rurdev.usda.gov/BCP_gar.html

Rural Business Enterprise Grants fund projects that facilitate the development of small and emerging rural businesses, distance learning networks, and employment-related adult education programs.

> www.rurdev.usda.gov/BCP_rbeg.html

Rural Business Opportunity Grants support training and technical assistance for business development and regional economic development planning. Collaborative economic planning and development through regional food systems is a specific focus.

     www.rurdev.usda.gov/BCP_RBOG.html

Rural Cooperative Development Grants support the creation or improvement of cooperative development centers that help start, enhance, or expand rural businesses, especially cooperatives.

     www.rurdev.usda.gov/BCP_RCDG.html

The Intermediary Relending Program provides loans to local organizations, or intermediaries, for the establishment of revolving loan funds. These revolving loan funds are used to finance business and economic development activity that creates or retains jobs in disadvantaged and remote communities. Intermediaries are encouraged to work in concert with State and regional strategies and in partnership with other public and private organizations that can provide complimentary resources.

     www.rurdev.usda.gov/BCP_irp.html

The Rural Microentrepreneur Assistance Program supports small business development in rural areas. Loans and grants are provided to Microenterprise Development Organizations which in turn provide loans and technical assistance to microentrepreneurs—including farmers—for developing their businesses. Loans may be used for working capital, debt refinancing, business acquisitions, and to purchase equipment or real estate, and grants support technical assistance and training. Nonprofit organizations, tribes, and public institutions of higher education that serve rural areas are eligible Microenterprise Development Organizations.

     www.rurdev.usda.gov/BCP_RMAP.html

Southwestern Wisconsin: Coordinating Multiple Funding Sources to Capitalize on Regional Assets

Southwestern Wisconsin regional and local leaders are combining multiple federal funding sources to strengthen the economy, create jobs, and capitalize on assets such as the strong agricultural sector. Through Project Produce, funded by a USDA Rural Business Opportunity Grant, they are exploring the feasibility of scaling up fruit and vegetable production on existing family farms and creating tools to help growers explore new markets in the region. This project was born out of a five county planning effort, Grow Southwest Wisconsin, which is funded by a HUD Sustainable Communities Regional Planning Grant and dedicated to making the area a place that the coming generations will want to live in. Several catalytic projects have also been implemented in the region. For instance, state brownfields funding, Scenic Byways funding, and a USDA Business & Industry Guaranteed Loan were used to revitalize the Potosi Brewery, a historic brewery along the Mississippi River that now provides jobs and serves as a tourist destination and local amenity.

Value Added Producer Grants support planning activities, such as business plan development, and provide working capital for value-added processing and marketing which helps farmers and ranchers receive a higher portion of the retail dollar. Specific funds are available for projects that focus on local and regional supply networks and support beginning farmers and ranchers, socially disadvantaged farmers and ranchers, and small- or medium-sized farms and ranches.

     www.rurdev.usda.gov/BCP_VAPG_Grants.html

Single Family Housing

USDA provides homeownership opportunities to low- and moderate-income rural Americans through several loan, grant, and loan guarantee programs targeted specifically to the needs of rural communities and households. The programs also offer funding to individuals to finance vital improvements that will make their homes decent, safe, and sanitary. Information on the following programs is available at www.rurdev.usda.gov/HSF_SFH.html.

- Rural Housing Direct and Guaranteed Loans support acquisition, construction, and repair.
- Rural Repair and Rehabilitation Loans and Grants support general repairs and improvements.
- Mutual Self-Help Loans help very low- and low-income households construct their own homes.
- Housing Application Packaging Grants help prepare applications for Housing and Community Facilities Programs.
- Self-Help Technical Assistance Grants help very low- and low-income households build homes using the self help method.
- Technical and Supervisory Assistance Grants assist low-income families in obtaining adequate housing and maintaining occupancy.

Multifamily Housing

USDA offers multifamily housing loans, loan guarantees, grants, and rental assistance. Some funds may also be used to buy and improve land and to provide necessary facilities such as water and waste disposal systems. Information on the following programs is available at www.rurdev.usda.gov/HMF_MFH.html.

- Rural Rental Housing Loans support new construction and rehabilitation.
- Guaranteed Rental Housing supports construction, acquisition, and rehabilitation.
- Housing Preservation Grants support repairs related to health and safety standards.
- Farm Labor Housing Loans and Grants support the construction or repair of farm labor housing.

Galesville, Wisconsin, courtesy of EPA

- The Rental Assistance Program provides rental assistance to households with incomes too low to pay the Housing and Community Facilities Program subsidized rent.

The Multifamily Housing Energy Efficiency Initiative, part of the existing multifamily application process, enables applicants to several Rural Development multifamily housing programs to enhance their eligibility for funding by incorporating energy efficiency practices into project design, construction, and operations. The Initiative's goal is to lower energy costs, reduce energy use, and decrease greenhouse gas emissions. Points are awarded to applicants who seek third-party energy efficiency certifications, use energy efficient building materials and design strategies, generate energy on site, and make a commitment to energy efficient post-construction operation and maintenance. Eligible programs are the Rural Rental Housing Program for New Construction, the Farm Labor Housing Loans and Farm Labor Housing Grants for Off-Farm Housing Programs, the Housing Preservation Grant Program, and the Multi-Family Housing Revitalization Demonstration Program.

Agriculture and Food

The Beginning Farmer and Rancher Development Program provides grants to organizations that train, educate, and provide outreach and technical assistance to new and beginning farmers on production, land management, marketing, business management, legal strategies, and other topics critical to running a successful operation.

www.nifa.usda.gov/funding/bfrdp/bfrdp.html

Small Business Innovation Research Grants help small businesses conduct research on scientific problems and opportunities in agriculture. Research is intended to increase the commercialization of agricultural innovations and foster participation by women-owned and socially and economically disadvantaged small businesses in technological development.

www.nifa.usda.gov/about/small_businesses.html

Specialty Crop Block Grants are awarded to state departments of agriculture to administer grant programs that enhance the competitiveness of specialty crops—fruits, vegetables, tree nuts, horticulture, nursery crops, and floriculture—including those that are locally grown and consumed. The program supports each state's specialty crop funding priorities, including state and local food systems, school and community gardens, farm-to-school programs, and improving access to specialty crops in underserved communities.

      www.ams.usda.gov/AMSv1.0/ams.fetchTemplateData.do?template=TemplateN&navID=SpecialtyCropBlockGrant%20Program&rightNav1=SpecialtyCropBlockGrant%20Program&topNav=&leftNav=&page=SCBGP&resultType=&acct=fvgrntprg

The Agriculture and Food Research Initiative supports research and education to support the viability of farms, small businesses, and community development initiatives.

      www.nifa.usda.gov/funding/afri/afri.html

- The Improved Sustainable Food Systems Program supports research, education, and project-specific efforts that will increase the security and viability of sustainable local and regional food.

- The Agricultural Economics and Rural Communities Program supports research, education, and project-specific efforts that enhance the long-term viability of small and medium-sized farms, small businesses and entrepreneurs, markets and trade, and rural communities broadly.

The Sustainable Agriculture Research and Education Program aims to advance sustainable innovations in agriculture. The program is managed by four regional offices that are guided by councils of local experts. The following types of grants are offered:

- Research and Education Grants: Ranging from $10,000 to $200,000 or more, these grants fund projects that involve scientists, producers, and others in an interdisciplinary approach.

- Professional Development Grants: Ranging from $20,000 to $120,000, these grants spread knowledge about sustainable practices by educating Cooperative Extension Service staff and other agricultural professionals.

- Producer Grants: These grants typically run between $1,000 and $15,000 to conduct research, marketing, and demonstration projects and share the results with other farmers and ranchers.

      www.nifa.usda.gov/sustainableagriculture.cfm

Previously funded Community Food Projects include:

- A community kitchen making value-added products in the Appalachian mountains of Tennessee;

- A revitalization of Native American dryland farming practices in the Sonoran Desert of Arizona;

- A pork producers' cooperative in rural Missouri marketing sustainably raised meat; and

- An urban agricultural center and farming enterprise among immigrants in Massachusetts.

Community Food Projects, supported by grants to nonprofit organizations, are designed to increase community food security by assessing strengths, establishing linkages, and creating systems that improve the self-reliance of community members over their food needs.

      www.nifa.usda.gov/fo/communityfoodprojects.cfm

The Farmers' Market Promotion Program provides grants to help communities support direct producer-to-consumer opportunities such as farmers' markets, roadside stands, community supported agriculture, and agritourism. Grants increase access to local foods by low-income consumers, allow growers to market their products directly to consumers, and raise awareness of local products through promotion and outreach.

Colorado, courtesy of NRCS

www.ams.usda.gov/AMSv1.0/ams.fetchTemplateData.do?template=TemplateN&navID=WholesaleandFarmersMarkets&leftNav=WholesaleandFarmersMarkets&page=FMPP&description=Farmers%20Market%20Promotion%20Program&acct=fmpp

The Federal-State Marketing Improvement Program provides grants to address barriers, challenges, and opportunities in marketing, transporting, and distributing food and forest products. State Departments of Agriculture are eligible recipients, but they often partner with local organizations, so see your State Department of Agriculture website for more information.

www.ams.usda.gov/AMSv1.0/ams.fetchTemplateData.do?template=TemplateC&navID=WholesaleandFarmersMarkets&leftNav=WholesaleandFarmersMarkets&page=FSMIP&description=Federal%20State%20Marketing%20Improvement%20Program&acct=gpfsmip

The Senior Farmers' Market Nutrition Program provides low-income seniors with coupons that can be exchanged for fruits, vegetables, herbs, and honey at farmers' markets, roadside stands, and community supported agriculture programs. Low-income seniors, generally defined as individuals who are at least 60 years old and who have household incomes less than 185% of the federal poverty level, are eligible.

www.fns.usda.gov/wic/seniorfmnp/sfmnpmenu.htm

The Women, Infants, and Children (WIC) Farmers' Market Nutrition Program aims to provide locally grown fruits and vegetables through farmers' markets to WIC participants and to expand their awareness and use of farmers' markets. Women, infants over 4 months old, and children under five years old who have been certified to receive WIC program benefits or who are on a waiting list for WIC certification are eligible.

www.fns.usda.gov/wic/FMNP/

Land Conservation

The Conservation Stewardship Program helps producers carry out activities that conserve or improve the quality of natural resources on their land, such as soil, water, air, and wildlife. The program shares the costs of implementing existing or new conservation activities. The sale of locally grown and marketed farm products is considered a conservation enhancement under this program.

Rappahannock County, Virginia, courtesy of EPA

    🖰   www.nrcs.usda.gov/wps/portal/nrcs/main/national/programs/financial/csp

Conservation Technical Assistance helps individuals manage natural resources such as soil, water, and wildlife. This program provides a broad array of assistance, including the conservation planning that must occur before an application for financial assistance from another program is approved and technical assistance to help individuals comply with regulatory requirements. No application is necessary; the program delivers assistance as needed to landowners, conservation districts, tribes, states, local jurisdictions, and others.

    🖰   www.nrcs.usda.gov/programs/cta

The Environmental Quality Incentives Program is a voluntary program that provides financial and technical assistance to agricultural producers through contracts of up to ten years in length. These contracts help plan and implement conservation practices that address natural resource concerns and that improve soil, water, plant, animal, air, and related resources on agricultural land and non-industrial private forestland. This program also helps producers meet federal, state, tribal, and local environmental regulations.

    🖰   www.nrcs.usda.gov/wps/portal/nrcs/main/national/programs/financial/eqip

The Farm and Ranch Land Protection Program's purpose is to keep agricultural lands in production, and it does this by assisting with the voluntary purchase of conservation easements from landowners. These easements ensure that the land will never be developed out of agricultural use and will continue to provide income for landowners. USDA partners with state, tribal, and local governments and farmland protection programs to acquire conservation easements from landowners. Owners of certain agricultural lands, subject to income limitations, apply through these state, tribal, and local entities.

    🖰   www.nrcs.usda.gov/wps/portal/nrcs/main/national/programs/easements/farmranch

The Forest Legacy Program from the U.S. Forest Service provides grants to state partners to protect important forests threatened by conversion. The program focuses on working forests that provide forest products and resource based jobs, protect air and water quality, provide recreational opportunities, and protect fish and wildlife habitat, including habitat of threatened or endangered species.

  🖱 www.fs.fed.us/cooperativeforestry/programs/loa/flp.shtml

The Forest Stewardship Program was established to encourage the long-term stewardship of nonindustrial private forest lands by assisting owners of those lands to more actively manage their forests. The program is delivered to landowners through a vast and effective network of forestry technical assistance providers, state forestry agencies, nonprofit partners, and others. The most prominent of these partners are the State Foresters, who link Forest Stewardship Program resources with the landowners in their states.

  🖱 www.fs.fed.us/cooperativeforestry/programs/loa/fsp.shtml

The Community Forest and Open Space Conservation Program provides financial assistance grants to local governments, tribes, and qualified nonprofit organizations to establish community forests. Communities and tribes can sustainably manage these community forests to achieve many public benefits, including recreation, income, wildlife habitat, stewardship demonstration sites, and environmental education.

  🖱 www.fs.fed.us/cooperativeforestry/programs/loa/cfp.shtml

Utilities and Energy Efficiency

USDA offers a variety of programs to support drinking water, sanitary sewer, solid waste, and storm drainage facilities in rural areas and cities and towns of 10,000 people or less. Information on these programs is available at www.rurdev.usda.gov/UWEP_HomePage.html.

- Water and Waste Loans and Grants support the construction or improvement of water and waste disposal systems.
- The Water and Waste Revolving Fund Program establishes lending programs to assist communities with water and wastewater systems.

The Rural Energy for America Program provides loan guarantees and grants to agricultural producers and small businesses in rural areas to purchase, install, and construct renewable energy systems; make energy efficiency improvements to non-residential buildings and facilities; use renewable technologies that reduce energy consumption; and participate in energy audits, renewable energy development assistance, and feasibility studies.

  🖱 www.rurdev.usda.gov/Energy.html

Appendix: Summary Matrix of Programs

This matrix contains summary information for the programs described in this guide. For complete details about each program, please visit the website provided in its description.

Program	Description of Assistance	Eligible Applicants	Match	CFDA #	Page #
HUD					
Community Planning and Development					5
Sustainable Communities Regional Planning Grants	Competitive grants of up to $5 million ($1.5 million for regions with under 200,000 people) for up to 36 months	Consortia of state and local governments, regional planning agencies, housing authorities, nonprofit organizations, tribal governments and organizations, and educational institutions	20%	14.703	5
Community Challenge Planning Grants	Competitive grants of up to $3 million (min. $100,000) for up to 36 months	State and local governments, tribes, public housing authorities, transit agencies, others	20%	14.704	5
Community Development Block Grants	Formula grants with competitive state allocation	Entitlement communities (such as metropolitan cities or urban counties). Allocated by states, typically competitively, to rural counties and non-entitlement communities	N/A	14.218	6
Section 108	Loan guarantees for up to five times the latest approved CDBG amount	CDBG entitlement recipients; non-entitlement communities can apply with state assistance	N/A	14.248	6
Choice Neighborhoods	Competitive grants for planning (up to $300,000) and implementation (up to $30 million)	Public housing authorities, local governments, tribal entities, nonprofits, and for-profit developers who apply jointly with a public entity	5%	14.889, 14.892	6
Section 242 Hospital Mortgage Insurance	Mortgage insurance	For-profit or nonprofit acute care (critical access) hospital facilities	N/A	14.128	7
Public Housing					7
Public Housing Program	Primarily formula grants, some competitive funding	Public housing authorities	N/A	14.850, 14.872	7
Housing Choice and Project-Based Vouchers	Formula grants	Public housing authorities	N/A	14.871, 14.195	7
Multifamily and Single Family Housing					8
HOME Investment Partnerships	Formula grants	States, cities, urban counties, and consortia. Other localities may apply for program funds made available by their state	25%	14.239	8
Mortgage Insurance for Rental Housing	Mortgage insurance	Eligible mortgagors include investors, builders, developers, and others who meet HUD requirements for mortgagors	N/A	14.134	8
Housing Finance Agency Risk Sharing Program	Mortgage insurance	Investors, builders, developers, public entities, and nonprofit corporations or associations may apply to a qualified HFA	N/A	14.188	9
Local Home Buying Programs	Consumer assistance (mortgage insurance, housing counseling, etc.)	Families and individuals	N/A	Various	9

Program	Description of Assistance	Eligible Applicants	Match	CFDA #	Page #
Multifamily and Single Family Housing					9
203(b) Mortgage Insurance	Mortgage insurance, eligible for approximately 96.5% financing	Families and individuals	N/A	14.117	9
203(k) Rehabilitation Mortgage Insurance	Mortgage insurance, eligible for approximately 96.5% financing	Individuals and families	N/A	14.108	9
Title I Home Improvement Loans	Loan guarantees of up to $25,000 for single-family homes	A property owner may apply at any approved lender	N/A	14.142	9
Home Mortgage and Foreclosure Counseling	Competitive grants (amount varies based on applicant category) to provide housing counseling	Applicants include HUD-approved housing-counseling agencies. Beneficiaries are tenants, homeowners, and homebuyers	N/A	14.169	9
Fair Housing					10
Fair Housing Initiatives	Competitive grants, amount varies based on initiative	Primarily fair housing organizations	N/A	14.408	10
Fair Housing Assistance	Noncompetitive grants related to administering fair housing laws	Fair housing enforcement organizations	N/A	14.401	10
Tribes					10
Indian Community Development Block Grants	Competitive grants with grant ceilings that vary by region	Eligible tribes or tribal organizations	N/A	14.886	10
Indian Housing Block Grants	Formula grants	Eligible tribes or tribally designated housing entities	N/A	14.867	10
Title VI Tribal Housing Activities Loan Guarantees	Loan guarantees up to 95%	Applicants are recipients of IHBG funding, beneficiaries are tribes and members	5%	14.869	10
Section 184 Indian Home Loan Guarantees	Loan guarantees for amounts up to 150% of the FHA lending limit for area	Tribes, tribally designated housing entities, and members of federally recognized tribes	N/A	14.865	11

Program	Description of Assistance	Eligible Applicants	Match	CFDA #	Page #
Supportive Housing for Target Populations					8
Mortgage Insurance for Residential Care Facilities	Mortgage insurance	Investors, builders, developers, public entities, nursing homes and private nonprofit corporations or associations	N/A	14.129	11
Section 202 Supportive Housing for the Elderly/Section 811 Supportive Housing for Persons with Disabilities	Competitive grants and noncompetitive contract renewal funding	Nonprofit organizations, which may partner with for-profit entities	N/A	14.157, 14.181	11
Housing Opportunities for Persons with AIDS	Formula funding and limited competitive grants	States, local government, and nonprofit organizations	N/A	14.241	11
Homeless Programs	Formula and competitive grants	States, local government, and nonprofit organizations	Varies	14.235, 14.238, 14.249	11
Healthy Homes					11
Lead Hazard Control Grants	Competitive grants of up to $2.3 million	States, tribes, local government	10%	14.900	11
DOT					12
Planning and Capacity Building					12
State Planning and Research	Technical assistance	State DOTs	20% with sliding scale	20.515	12
FHWA/FTA Transportation Planning Capacity Building	Technical assistance	MPOs, state DOTs, local governments, national stakeholders	N/A		12
Surface Transportation Environment and Planning Cooperative Research	Technical assistance	MPOs, state DOTs, local governments, national stakeholders, universities, nonprofits	50%		12

Program	Description of Assistance	Eligible Applicants	Match	CFDA #	Page #
Multimodal Transportation					13
Transportation Investment Generating Economic Recovery (TIGER) Grants	Competitive grants	Funding goes directly to State DOTs and local government agencies based on grant application process	20% urban; none rural	20.932	13
Surface Transportation Program	Apportionment formula grants	Highway Trust Funds are apportioned by formula to state DOTs. Each state then carries out a statewide planning process that includes consultation with non-metropolitan local officials to develop a Statewide Transportation Improvement Plan. 10% of funds are set aside for safety, 10% for transportation enhancement activities, 50% are divided between urbanized areas over 200,000 in population and the remaining areas of the state, and the rest can be used in any area of the state	20% with sliding scale	20.932	13
Congestion Mitigation and Air Quality Program	Apportionment formula grants	Highway Trust Funds are apportioned by formula to state DOTs. Each state then carries out a statewide planning process. A metropolitan planning organization or state can partner with any public, private, or nonprofit entity to implement any funded project	20% with sliding scale	20.205	13
Public Lands Highways	Competitive grants	Allocated directly to federal land management agencies (National Park Service, U.S. Fish and Wildlife Service, National Forest Service, Bureau of Land Management) which then distribute competitive grants to state DOTs	N/A		13
Recreational Trails	Apportionment formula grants	Apportioned by formula to state natural resources or parks agencies, which then distribute funding to local governments	20% with sliding scale	20.219	14
Transportation Enhancements	Apportionment formula grants	Surface Transportation Program funds are set aside in each state (see above). Each state develops its own procedures to solicit and select projects for funding	20% with sliding scale		14
Safe Routes to School	Apportionment formula grants	Apportioned by formula to state DOTs, which then distribute funding to state, local, and regional agencies and nonprofit organizations	N/A		14
Public Transit					14
Formula Grants for Other than Urbanized Areas (5311)	Apportionment formula grants	Apportioned by formula to state DOTs, which then distribute funding using their own formulas and selection criteria to local governments, nonprofits, and transit operators in rural areas with populations less than 50,000	20% capital; 50% operational	20.509	14
Paul S. Sarbanes Transit in the Parks Grants	Competitive grants	Federal land management agencies; state, tribal, and local governments with jurisdiction over land in an eligible area	Up to 100%	20.520	14
Bus and Bus Facilities Grants	Competitive grants	State and local governments	20% capital	20.500	15
Rural Transit Assistance Program	Apportionment formula grants	State RTAP funds are apportioned by formula to state DOTs, with $65,000 going to each state and Puerto Rico, $10,000 to other territories, and the balance distributed according to each state's nonurbanized population. Funds are then distributed to local governments and transit providers	N/A	20.509	15

Program	Description of Assistance	Eligible Applicants	Match	CFDA #	Page #
Streets and Highways					15
Transportation, Community, and System Preservation Program	Competitive grants	States, metropolitan planning organizations, local governments, tribal governments	20% with sliding scale		15
Interstate Maintenance	Apportionment formula grants	Apportioned by formula to state DOTs	10%		16
Highway Safety Improvement Program	Apportionment formula grants	Apportioned by formula to state DOTs, which may use funds or distribute them to local governments	10% with sliding scale		16
Highway Bridge Program	Apportionment formula grants	Apportioned by formula to state DOTs, which may use funds or distribute them to local governments	20%; 10% on Inter-states		16
National Scenic Byways	Competitive grants	State DOTs	20%		16
High Risk Rural Roads Program	Apportionment formula grants	Apportioned by formula to state DOTs, which in most cases use funds directly, but can also distribute them to local agencies based on need	10% with sliding scale		16
Tribes					17
Public Transportation on Indian Reservations Grants	Competitive grants	Tribes	N/A	20.590	17
Supportive Services for Target Populations					17
Transportation for Elderly Persons and Persons with Disabilities	Apportionment formula grants	Apportioned by formula to state DOTs, which then distribute funding to local governments	20% capital	20.513	17
Job Access and Reverse Commute Program	Apportionment formula grants	Apportioned by formula to state DOTs, which then distribute funding to other public bodies	20% capital; 50% oper-ational	20.516	17
New Freedom Grants	Apportionment formula grants	Apportioned by formula to state DOTs, which then distribute funding to other public bodies	20% capital; 50% oper-ational	20.521	17
National Resource Center for Human Service Transportation Coordination	Technical assistance	States, local governments, and public and private providers	N/A	20.514	17
National Center on Senior Transportation	Technical assistance and competitive demonstration grants	States, local governments, and public and private providers	N/A	20.514	17
Easter Seals Project ACTION	Technical assistance	States, local governments, and public and private providers	N/A	20.514	18

					18
Supportive Services for Target Populations					
National Joblinks Employment Transportation Initiative	Technical assistance	States, local governments, and public and private providers	N/A	20.514	18
EPA					19
Community Planning					19
Smart Growth Implementation Assistance	Technical assistance from national experts over 18-month period	State, local, regional, and tribal governments; nonprofits that have partnered with a governmental entity	N/A		19
Building Blocks for Sustainable Communities	One-day technical assistance workshop	Local, county, and tribal governments	N/A		19
Governors' Institute on Community Design®	Two-day technical assistance workshop	Governors and their cabinet members	N/A		19
Brownfields Cleanup and Redevelopment					20
Brownfields Assessment Grants	Competitive grants of up to $200,000	State, local, and tribal governments; general purpose units of local government, land clearance authorities, or other quasi-governmental entities; regional councils or redevelopment agencies; states or legislatures	N/A	66.818	21
Brownfields Cleanup Grants	Competitive grants of up to $200,000	State, local, and tribal governments; general purpose units of local government, land clearance authorities, or other quasi-governmental entities; regional councils or redevelopment agencies; states or legislatures; nonprofit organizations	20% (money, labor, material, or services); applicants can request a waiver	66.818	21
Brownfields Revolving Loan Fund Grants	Competitive grants of up to $1,000,000	State, local, and tribal governments; general purpose units of local government, land clearance authorities, or other quasi-governmental entities; regional councils or redevelopment agencies; states or legislatures	20% (money, labor, material, or services); applicants can request a waiver	66.818	21
Brownfields State and Tribal Response Program	Noncompetitive grants	States; tribes	N/A, unless capitalizing an RLF	66.817	22
Brownfields Area-Wide Planning Grants	Competitive grants and technical assistance worth up to $175,000	General purpose units of local government, land clearance authorities, or other quasi-governmental entities; regional councils or groups of general purpose units of local government; redevelopment agencies; tribal governments; nonprofit organizations	N/A	66.814	22
Brownfields Environmental Workforce Development and Job Training Grants	Competitive grants of up to $200,000	State, local, and tribal governments; general purpose units of local government, land clearance authorities, or other quasi-governmental entities; regional councils or redevelopment agencies; states or legislatures; nonprofit organizations	N/A	66.815	22
Targeted Brownfields Assessments	Technical assistance worth up to $100,000	State, local, and tribal governments; general purpose units of local government, land clearance authorities, or other quasi-governmental entities; regional councils or redevelopment agencies; states or legislatures; nonprofit organizations	N/A		22
Technical Assistance to Brownfields Communities	Technical assistance	State, local, and tribal governments, regional councils, and others	N/A		22

Program	Description of Assistance	Eligible Applicants	Match	CFDA #	Page #
Water Infrastructure and Water Quality					23
Clean Water State Revolving Fund	Loans	EPA apportions funds to states, which provide loans to communities, individuals, and nonprofit organizations	States: 20% of federal appropriation; assistance recipient: none	66.458	23
Drinking Water State Revolving Fund	Loans, grants (very limited availability), technical assistance through set-aside funding	EPA awards funds to states, which provide loans to publicly and privately owned community water systems and nonprofit non-community water systems	States: 20% of federal appropriation; assistance recipient: none	66.468	23
U.S.-Mexico Border Water Infrastructure Program Grants	Competitive grants	Communities within 100 km north and south of the U.S.-Mexico Border	U.S.: none; Mexico: yes	66.202	23
Nonpoint Source Implementation Grants	Formula grants	EPA apportions funds to state and tribal agencies, which can provide funds to local governments, tribal authorities, regional development centers, school systems, colleges and universities, nonprofit organizations, for-profit groups, individuals, and others	40%	66.460	23
Pollution Control Grant Program (Clean Water Act Section 106)	Formula grants	States, interstate agencies, tribes	Tribes: 5% (can include in-kind)	66.419	23
Tribes					24
Alaska Native Village and Rural Communities Sanitation Grants	Competitive grants	EPA provides funds to the Alaska Department of Environmental Conservation which distributes the funds to rural and tribal communities using a priority list	N/A	66.202	24
Clean Water Indian Set-Aside Program	Competitive grants	EPA selects projects using Indian Health Service priority lists	N/A	66.418	24
U.S.-Mexico Tribal Border Infrastructure Grants	Competitive grants of $250,000 to $500,000 on average	Tribes whose reservations are within 100 km north of the U.S.-Mexico border	N/A	66.202	24
Environmental Justice					24
Environmental Justice Small Grants Program	Competitive grants	Nonprofit community-based organizations, tribal governments, and tribal organizations	N/A	66.604	25
Environmental Justice Collaborative Problem-Solving Cooperative Agreements	Competitive grants of approximately $100,000	Nonprofit organizations			25
Healthy Buildings					25
State Indoor Radon Grant Program	Grants—total annual appropriation of $8 million	States, tribes	40%	66.032	25
Energy Efficiency					25
Local Climate and Energy Program	Technical assistance—web-based informational resources and analytical tools	Resources are free and available to any interested local governments and their partners	N/A		25
ENERGY STAR for New Homes	Certification program	Builders partner with EPA	N/A		25

Program	Description of Assistance	Eligible Applicants	Match	CFDA #	Page #
USDA					26
Community and Economic Development					26
Community Facilities	Loans, loan guarantees, and grants	Public entities, tribal governments, and nonprofit corporations in communities with populations up to 20,000	N/A	10.776	26
Rural Community Development Initiative	Grants, technical assistance	Intermediaries can be public or private organizations. Recipients of assistance from the intermediary can be nonprofit organizations, low-income communities, and tribes	N/A	10.446	26
Business Development					26
Business and Industry Guaranteed Loan Program	Loan guarantees	Public, tribal, and private entities in communities with populations up to 50,000	N/A	10.768	26
Rural Business Enterprise Grants	Grants, technical assistance worth $25,000-$500,000 (average $100,000)	State agencies; local governments, tribal governments, and nonprofit corporations in communities with populations up to 50,000		10.769	2
Rural Business Opportunity Grants	Grants, technical assistance varying in size; recent ranged from $10,000-$250,000	State agencies; local governments, tribal governments, and nonprofit corporations in communities with populations up to 50,000		10.773	27
Rural Cooperative Development Grants	Grants	Non-profits or institutions of higher education serving areas with populations up to 50,000	25%	10.771	27
Intermediary Relending Program	Loans to establish revolving loan funds	Intermediaries can be nonprofit corporations, public and tribal governments, and cooperatives. Assistance recipients can be individuals, nonprofits, public bodies, and others in communities with populations up to 25,000	N/A	10.767	27
Rural Microentrepreneur Assistance Program	Loans and grants to intermediary organizations	Microenterprise development organizations in areas with populations up to 50,000	15%		27
Value Added Producer Grants	Grants	Independent producers, cooperatives, and producer-controlled business groups	50%	10.352	28
Single Family Housing					28
Rural Housing Direct and Guaranteed Loans	Loans, loan guarantees	Very low- and low-income households in communities with populations up to 20,000		10.410	28
Rural Repair and Rehabilitation Loans and Grants	Loans, grants	Very low- and low-income households in communities with populations up to 20,000		10.417, 10.444	28
Mutual Self-Help Loans	Loans, technical assistance	Public bodies, tribes, and non-profits serving very low- and low-income households in communities with populations up to 20,000		10.411, 10.420	28
Housing Application Packaging Grants	Grants	Tax-exempt public agencies and private non-profit organizations			28
Self-Help Technical Assistance Grants	Grants, technical assistance	Intermediaries can be states, political subdivisions, private or public nonprofit corporations. Assistance recipients are very low- and low-income households		10.420	28
Technical and Supervisory Assistance Grants	Grants, technical assistance	Intermediaries can be public or private nonprofit corporations, agencies, institutions, organizations, tribes, and other associations. Assistance recipients are low-income families			28

Program	Description of Assistance	Eligible Applicants	Match	CFDA #	Page #
Multifamily Housing					28
Rural Rental Housing Loans	Loans	Public bodies, tribes, and non-profits serving very low- and low-income households in communities with populations up to 20,000		10.415, 10.438	28
Guaranteed Rental Housing	Guaranteed loans	Private and public lenders			28
Housing Preservation Grants	Grants to relend or regrant to homeowners	Public bodies, tribes, and non-profits serving very low- and low-income households in communities with populations up to 20,000		10.433	28
Farm Labor Housing Loans and Grants	Loans, grants	Farmers and related organizations		10.405	28
Rental Assistance Program	Project-based subsidy	Existing Rural Development multifamily borrowers	N/A	10.427	29
Agriculture and Food					29
Beginning Farmer and Rancher Development Program	Technical assistance, education, and outreach	State, tribal, and local entities and regional organizations and partnerships	25%	10.311	29
Small Business Innovation Research Grants	Grants	Small businesses		10.212	29
Specialty Crop Block Grants	Grants	State Departments of Agriculture		10.170	30
Agriculture and Food Research Initiative	Competitive grants	Institutions of higher education		10.310	30
Sustainable Agriculture Research and Education Program	Competitive grants of $1,000-$200,000	Non-profits and individuals		10.215	30
Community Food Projects	Grants, technical assistance	Intermediaries are non-profit organizations		10.225	30
Farmers' Market Promotion Program	Grants	Non-profit organizations, tribal, and local governments; economic development entities		10.163	31
Federal-State Marketing Improvement Program	Grants	State Departments of Agriculture		10.156	31
Senior Farmers' Market Nutrition Program	Vouchers	Low-income seniors (programs managed by state agencies)	N/A	10.576	31
Women, Infants, and Children Farmers' Market Nutrition Program	Vouchers	WIC-eligible women and children (programs managed by state agencies)	N/A	10.572	31
Land Conservation					32
Conservation Stewardship Program	Land use payments for environmental benefits produced	Farm and ranch owners and operators		10.924	32
Conservation Technical Assistance	Technical assistance provided directly by NRCS staff	Farm and ranch owners and operators		10.902	32
Environmental Quality Incentives Program	Financial assistance payments, technical assistance	Farm and ranch owners and operators			32
Farm and Ranch Land Protection Program	Matching funds to purchase conservation easements	State, tribal, and local governments and non-governmental organizations	50% of easement market value		32

Program	Description of Assistance	Eligible Applicants	Match	CFDA #	Page #
Forest Legacy Program	Grants	State agencies identified by governors as lead agencies for the program	25%	10.676	33
Forest Stewardship Program	Grants	State forestry or equivalent agency	Determined by Forest Service regional/ area office	10.678	33
Community Forest and Open Space Conservation Program	Grants	Local governmental entities, tribes, qualified nonprofit organizations	50%	10.689	33
Utilities and Energy Efficiency					33
Water and Waste Loans and Grants	Loans, grants	Public bodies, tribes, and non-profits in communities with populations up to 10,000		10.760	33
Water and Waste Revolving Fund Program	Grants to establish revolving loan funds	Non-profit organizations in communities with populations up to 10,000		10.862	33
Rural Energy for America Program	Loan guarantees, grants	Small businesses; agricultural producers; state, tribal, and local governments; and institutions of higher education in communities with populations up to 50,000	75%	10.868	33